"What couple hasn't struggled from time to time with praying together? *When Couples Pray* is a must-read for any husband and wife who desire a closer relationship with each other. Read, let it sink into your heart, and experience a oneness with your mate and God like you've never experienced before!"

DR. GARY AND BARBARA ROSBERG
HOSTS OF *AMERICA'S FAMILY COACHES...LIVE!* AND
COAUTHORS, *THE 5 LOVE NEEDS OF MEN AND WOMEN*

"It's always nice to know we're not alone in our marriage struggles, that someone understands, and that answers can be found. Cheri Fuller's easy-to-read book comes alongside in just this way. Readers can identify with and apply godly truths to solving similar challenges as they strengthen their Christian homes."

LYNDA HUNTER BJORKLUND
AUTHOR, SPEAKER, SYNDICATED COLUMNIST

"*When Couples Pray* is not another guilt-charged book chiding couples on the need to pray together. Loaded with encouragement, *When Couples Pray* shows in a 'come-alongside way' both the struggles and results of couples who began praying together. Speaking as a typical man who is not naturally driven to intimacy, *When Couples Pray* made me want to initiate this practice in my own marriage. I heartily recommend this book to you; it will make a difference in your marriage."

JONATHAN GRAF
EDITOR, *PRAY!* MAGAZINE

Also by Cheri Fuller

WHEN COUPLES PRAY

The Little-Known Secret
to Lifelong
Happiness in Marriage

Multnomah® Publishers *Sisters, Oregon*

CHERI FULLER

WHEN COUPLES PRAY

published by Multnomah Publishers, Inc.
in association with the literary agency of Alive Communications, Inc.
7680 Goddard Street, Suite 200, Colorado Springs, CO 80920

© 2001 by Cheri Fuller
International Standard Book Number: 1-57673-666-0

Cover image by Christine Alicino/Photonica

Scripture quotations are from:
The Holy Bible, New International Version © 1973, 1984 by International Bible Society,
used by permission of Zondervan Publishing House

Also quoted:
The Holy Bible, New King James Version (NKJV) © 1984 by Thomas Nelson, Inc.
The Living Bible (TLB) © 1971. Used by permission of Tyndale House Publishers, Inc.
All rights reserved.
The Message © 1993 by Eugene H. Peterson
The New Testament in Modern English, Revised Edition (Phillips)
© 1958, 1960, 1972 by J. B. Phillips
The Amplified Bible (AMP) © 1965, 1987 by Zondervan Publishing House.
Holy Bible, New Living Translation (NLT) © 1996. Used by permission of
Tyndale House Publishers, Inc. All rights reserved.
New American Standard Bible (NASB) © 1960, 1977 by The Lockman Foundation

Multnomah is a trademark of Multnomah Publishers, Inc.
and is registered in the U.S. Patent and Trademark Office.
The colophon is a trademark of Multnomah Publishers, Inc.

For information:
MULTNOMAH PUBLISHERS, INC.•POST OFFICE BOX 1720•SISTERS, OREGON 97759

Library of Congress Cataloging-in-Publication Data
Fuller, Cheri. When couples pray : the little known secret to lifelong
happiness in marriage / by Cheri Fuller. p.cm.
Includes bibliographical references. ISBN 1-57673-666-0 (pbk.)
1. Spouses—Religious life. 2. Prayer—Christianity. 3. Marriage—Religious
aspects—Christianity. I. Title. BV4596.M3 F85 2001 248.8'44—dc21 00-011255

02 03 04 05 06 — 10 9 8 7 6 5 4 3 2 1

To Holmes

prayer partner, faithful husband, marvelous father, best friend.

Acknowledgments

A book is not written in a vacuum. It's a team effort, and I want to thank the team who helped make this book a reality. Jeff Leeland planted the seed; Dee Brestin watered it and encouraged me greatly. Dan Benson and Nancy Thompson, my terrific editors, Bill Jensen, and the Multnomah team brought the project into full bloom. Thank you! My heartfelt thanks also to Greg Johnson, my agent, for his support and encouragement and to all those couples who shared their stories of what happened when they prayed. My thanks wouldn't be complete without including my husband, Holmes, for being my companion on this spiritual journey and for being so willing all those times I said, "Honey, let's pray."

CONTENTS